W0081535

THE CAVE PEOPLE OF THE
Karawari
A DISAPPEARING CULTURE

by Jennifer Carlson

NATIONAL
GEOGRAPHIC
LEARNING

CENGAGE
Learning·

Deep in the jungle of the Karawari region of Papua New Guinea, high in the hills above the Arafundi and Karawari rivers, live an amazing people called the Meakambut.

The Meakambut are nomadic. This means they do not live in one place all the time. Instead, they move from place to place, carrying everything they own with them. They live the way that their people have lived for thousands of years—far from the modern world, and with very little help from outsiders.

There are barely 50 Meakambut men, women, and children. They live in an area of jungle in the mountains that is about 10 miles wide and 10 miles long. They live in this area, moving between different caves, rock shelters, and simple man-made shelters.

Many years ago, there were other groups who also lived in caves in the Karawari. But they all left the caves in the mountains and went to live in villages. The Meakambut are the only people still living in these caves.

Indonesia

Papua New Guinea

Australia

3

There are over 300 caves and rock shelters in the Karawari. Many of them belong to the Meakambut. It is a tradition for each cave to have a name and an owner. The caves are passed down from father to son. The Meakambut often tell stories and legends about the caves. And many of the caves have paintings on the walls that tell about the Meakambut people.

For generations, the Meakambut have made handprints on the walls of the caves. They have made the handprints using paint made from clay. Some of the handprints are new, and some are very old. Some may be up to 20,000 years old!

There are handprints like these in ancient caves in other parts of the world, too.

The Meakambut move quickly with their bare feet over stones and through the jungle vines. They know the land very well. This is important because they must find food in the jungle.

They gather wild fruits and other plants. They plant some foods, like bananas and pumpkins, and pick them up when they pass the same place again. The men use handcrafted spears, knives, and bows and arrows to hunt for birds, wild pigs, fish, and other animals.

The Meakambuts' main food is called sago. It is a starch from the inside of the sago palm tree. Getting the sago starch out of the tree is very hard work, and the community must cooperate to do it. Later, they make pancakes with the sago and cook the pancakes over a fire. The Meakambut build fires by rubbing a strip of bamboo against a stick.

Meakambut men wear a loincloth. Traditionally, the loincloths are made with leaves. The women wear grass skirts. Sometimes, though, the Meakambut wear modern cloth skirts, T-shirts, and shorts that they receive through trade or donations.

The Meakambut also decorate their faces and bodies. They use leaves to create headdresses, and sometimes also fur, feathers, or flowers. They wear necklaces made of shells.

Painting their faces and bodies is the Meakambut way of getting "dressed up."

The Meakambut people are proud of their culture and their traditions. Holding on to their land and their old way of life is important to the Meakambut, but they face many difficulties.

The Meakambut are very far from towns and cities. So they must travel far over the mountains or down the river to get to the nearest clinics. Sometimes healthy people must carry sick people on their backs.

There are also companies that want to cut down the jungle trees for wood and to mine the land for metals.

Nancy Sullivan, an American anthropologist, and a team of Papua New Guinean researchers are working with the Meakambut to write down the location and history of the Meakambut caves and to photograph the paintings. They hope this will bring attention to the Meakambut culture, and that this will make the government want to preserve the caves and the land.

Sullivan's team is also working on getting basic help for the Meakambut, such as doctors' visits and building materials.

The Meakambut worry about their future. Many of them believe that leaving their caves to settle in villages and grow gardens may be the best way forward, even though that would mean giving up some of their traditions.

With the help of Nancy Sullivan's team, the Meakambut started a new village called Tembakapa. They still move from place to place, but not as much as before. They hope their government will now help them build homes, a health clinic, and a school.

As long as the Meakambut survive, their culture and their history will survive, too.

Facts About Traditional Headdresses

People in many cultures around the world wear headdresses. Headdresses are coverings that hide and decorate the head. In the past, some groups wore headdresses every day. Today, many groups wear them only for special celebrations.

A Headdress from Australia

In Australia's aboriginal communities, men wear tall headdresses for important celebrations. These tall headdresses are made with twigs and hair, then decorated using emu feathers and a wild plant called wamurlu.

A Headdress from India

During festivals, married women in parts of India wear a colorful headdress called a perak. Rows of turquoise and coral beads are attached to wool on this heavy, hand-crafted headdress, which is often passed from mother to daughter. According to tradition, the more beads on a perak, the more money a woman has.

A Headdress from Nigeria

A headdress called a gele is part of the traditional dress of Yoruba women in Nigeria. A gele is made by winding one large piece of stiff cloth around a woman's head. In the Yoruba culture, the direction a gele leans tells whether or not the wearer is married. Today, many other African women wear geles as part of their everyday dress, but the direction they lean is not always a sign of whether they are married.

◄ Australian aboriginal headdress

▲ Nigerian gele

◄ Indian perak

13

Word Play

Community and Culture

Write the correct word next to each definition.

community proud culture tradition generation

____culture____ the ideas, activities, and ways of behaving that are special to a country, people, or region

_____ any of the different age levels in a family, such as grandparents, children, and grandchildren

_____ pleased with an accomplishment

_____ the passing of customs and beliefs from one generation to another

_____ the people as a group in a town, city, or other area

Write the word for each picture. Then, on a separate piece of paper, write sentences using each word.

generations   handcrafted   proud   community

handcrafted

Glossary

anthropologist a person who studies humans and their culture

arrows weapons shot from a bow and usually having a pointed head and feathers at the other end

bamboo a plant with long, hollow stems

bows weapons for shooting arrows, usually made of a curved piece of wood and a string tied to both ends

clinics places where people go for medical services

donations gifts that others make to people who are in need of the gifts

emu a large Australian bird that does not fly

headdresses coverings or decorations for the head

loincloth a cloth wrapped around the hips, worn by men in some hot areas as their only piece of clothing

preserve to protect from harm and keep in good condition for a long time

spears long sticks with sharp tips for hunting and killing animals

starch a white, powdery substance that is found in foods like rice, potatoes, pasta, and bread

turquoise a blue-green stone often used to decorate things and to make jewelry